BY ALLAN MOREY

THE GREEN BAY
PACKERS
STORY

TORQUE

BELLWETHER MEDIA · MINNEAPOLIS, MN

TM

Are you ready to take it to the extreme? Torque books thrust you into the action-packed world of sports, vehicles, mystery, and adventure. These books may include dirt, smoke, fire, and chilling tales. **WARNING** : read at your own risk.

This edition first published in 2017 by Bellwether Media, Inc.

No part of this publication may be reproduced in whole or in part without written permission of the publisher. For information regarding permission, write to Bellwether Media, Inc., Attention: Permissions Department, 5357 Penn Avenue South, Minneapolis, MN 55419.

Library of Congress Cataloging-in-Publication Data

Names: Morey, Allan.
Title: The Green Bay Packers Story / by Allan Morey.
Description: Minneapolis, MN : Bellwether Media, Inc., 2017. | Series:
  Torque: NFL Teams | Includes bibliographical references and index.
Identifiers: LCCN 2015034271 | ISBN 9781626173668 (hardcover : alk. paper)
Subjects: LCSH: Green Bay Packers (Football team)–History–Juvenile
  literature.
Classification: LCC GV956.G7 M67 2017 | DDC 796.332/640977561–dc23
LC record available at http://lccn.loc.gov/2015034271

Printed in the United States of America, North Mankato, MN.

TABLE OF CONTENTS

Quarterback Aaron Rodgers has the ball. He drops back to pass. He slings the ball to **wide receiver** Greg Jennings. Jennings catches the pass at the end zone. Touchdown!

STAR OF THE GAME
Aaron Rodgers was voted Most Valuable Player (MVP) of Super Bowl 45.

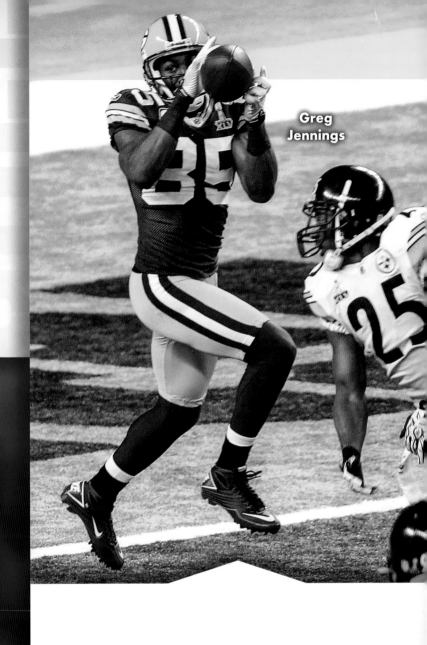

Greg
Jennings

The Green Bay Packers now lead the Pittsburgh Steelers 21 to 3 in Super Bowl 45. But the game is far from over.

The Steelers come roaring back. Late in the game, the score is close. The Packers' lead is only 28 to 25.

But the ball is in Rodgers' hands again. He throws a long pass to Jennings. The catch keeps the **offense** alive. Soon the Packers kick a field goal. They go on to win 31 to 25!

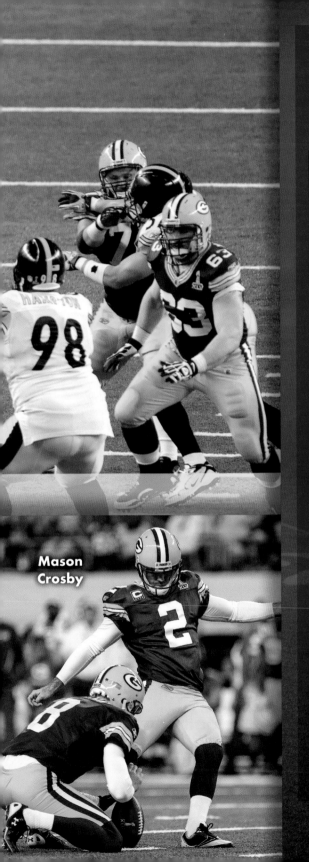

Mason Crosby

SCORING TERMS

END ZONE
the area at each end of a football field; a team scores by entering the opponent's end zone with the football.

EXTRA POINT
a score that occurs when a kicker kicks the ball between the opponent's goal posts after a touchdown is scored; 1 point.

FIELD GOAL
a score that occurs when a kicker kicks the ball between the opponent's goal posts; 3 points.

SAFETY
a score that occurs when a player on offense is tackled behind his own goal line; 2 points for defense.

TOUCHDOWN
a score that occurs when a team crosses into its opponent's end zone with the football; 6 points.

TWO-POINT CONVERSION
a score that occurs when a team crosses into its opponent's end zone with the football after scoring a touchdown; 2 points.

The Packers have won more championships than any other American football team. This has earned Green Bay, Wisconsin, the nickname "Titletown, USA."

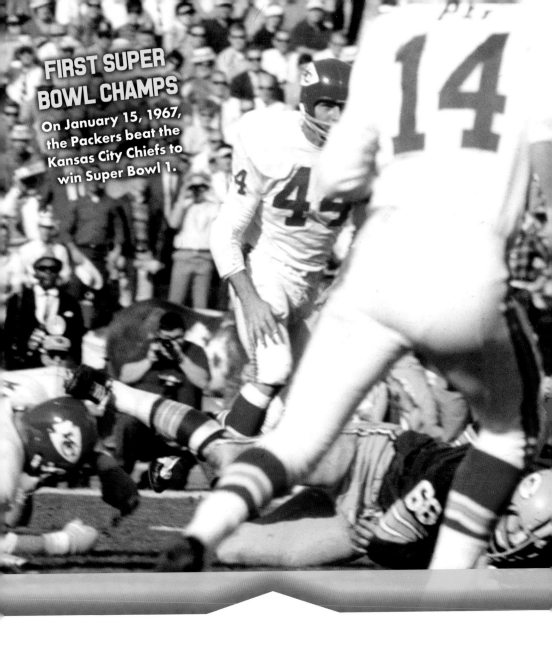

The Packers brought home their first championship in 1929. They went on to win eight more National Football League (NFL) titles before Super Bowl games were even played!

Green Bay is the smallest United States city with a professional sports team. Just over 100,000 people live there.

The Packers play at Lambeau Field. The stadium was named after Earl "Curly" Lambeau. He cofounded and coached the team. Opened in 1957, Lambeau Field is one of the oldest stadiums in the NFL.

Earl "Curly" Lambeau

SNOW CREW
Sometimes Lambeau Field gets covered in snow. Fans show up to shovel snow from the stands.

LAMBEAU FIELD

GREEN BAY, WISCONSIN

LAMBEAU FIELD

The Packers have a long history. They joined the NFL in 1921. Today, they play in the North **Division** of the National Football **Conference** (NFC).

The North Division is nicknamed the "Black and Blue Division." It has some tough **rivalries**. The Packers battle the Chicago Bears, Minnesota Vikings, and Detroit Lions.

NFL DIVISIONS

AFC

AFC **NORTH**

 BALTIMORE **RAVENS**

 CINCINNATI **BENGALS**

 CLEVELAND **BROWNS**

 PITTSBURGH **STEELERS**

AFC **EAST**

BUFFALO **BILLS**

MIAMI **DOLPHINS**

NEW ENGLAND **PATRIOTS**

 NEW YORK **JETS**

AFC **SOUTH**

 HOUSTON **TEXANS**

 INDIANAPOLIS **COLTS**

 JACKSONVILLE **JAGUARS**

 TENNESSEE **TITANS**

AFC **WEST**

 DENVER **BRONCOS**

 KANSAS CITY **CHIEFS**

 OAKLAND **RAIDERS**

 SAN DIEGO **CHARGERS**

REGULAR RIVALS

No other teams have played each other as many times as the Packers and Bears.

NFC

NFC NORTH

CHICAGO
BEARS

DETROIT
LIONS

GREEN BAY
PACKERS

MINNESOTA
VIKINGS

NFC EAST

DALLAS
COWBOYS

NEW YORK
GIANTS

PHILADELPHIA
EAGLES

WASHINGTON
REDSKINS

NFC SOUTH

ATLANTA
FALCONS

CAROLINA
PANTHERS

NEW ORLEANS
SAINTS

TAMPA BAY
BUCCANEERS

NFC WEST

ARIZONA
CARDINALS

LOS ANGELES
RAMS

SAN FRANCISCO
49ERS

SEATTLE
SEAHAWKS

Lambeau helped start the Packers in 1919. He went on to coach the team for 31 seasons. He led the Packers to six NFL Championships.

After Lambeau, the Packers struggled. But then in 1959, Vince Lombardi became the team's coach. He led the Packers to win five championships. He was around for the first two Super Bowls.

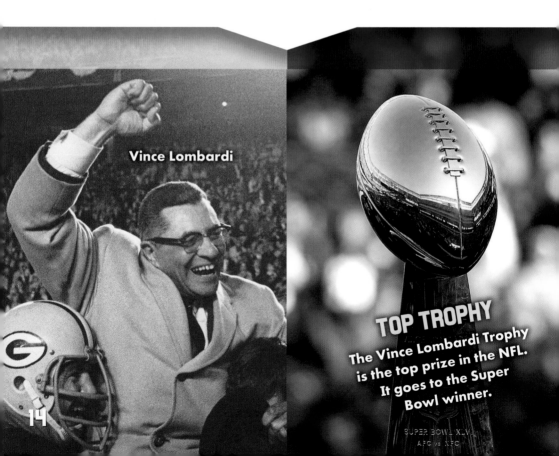

Vince Lombardi

TOP TROPHY
The Vince Lombardi Trophy is the top prize in the NFL. It goes to the Super Bowl winner.

In the 1970s and 1980s, the Packers lost a lot. But that changed in 1992. Quarterback Brett Favre joined the team.

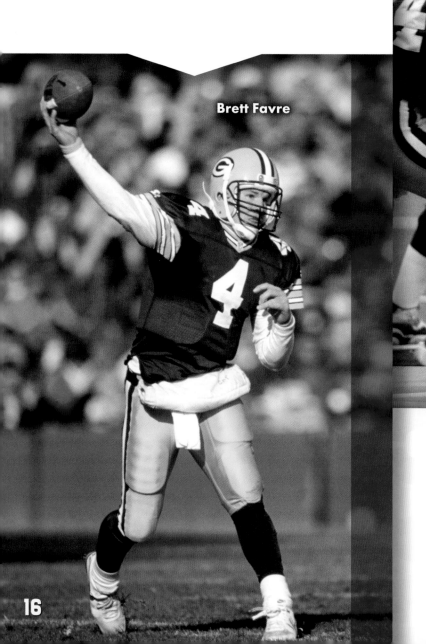

Brett Favre

After the 1996 season, Favre led the Packers to win Super Bowl 31. Even after Favre left, the team has done well. They continue to make the **playoffs** most years.

TIMELINE

1919

Cofounded by Earl "Curly" Lambeau and George Calhoun

1929

Won their first NFL Championship by having the best record in the league

1921

Joined the NFL

1957

First played at Lambeau Field

Won Super Bowl 2, beating
the Oakland Raiders

33 FINAL SCORE **14**

2011

Won Super Bowl 45, beating
the Pittsburgh Steelers

31 FINAL SCORE **25**

1997

Won Super Bowl 31, beating
the New England Patriots

35 FINAL SCORE **21**

1967

Won Super Bowl 1, beating
the Kansas City Chiefs

35 FINAL SCORE **10**

1992

Welcomed Hall-of-Fame
quarterback Brett Favre

2005

Drafted quarterback
Aaron Rodgers

2009

Drafted linebacker Clay Matthews

PACKERS

Many great quarterbacks have played for the Packers. Long before Favre, Bart Starr had the role. He led the team to win the NFL's first two Super Bowls.

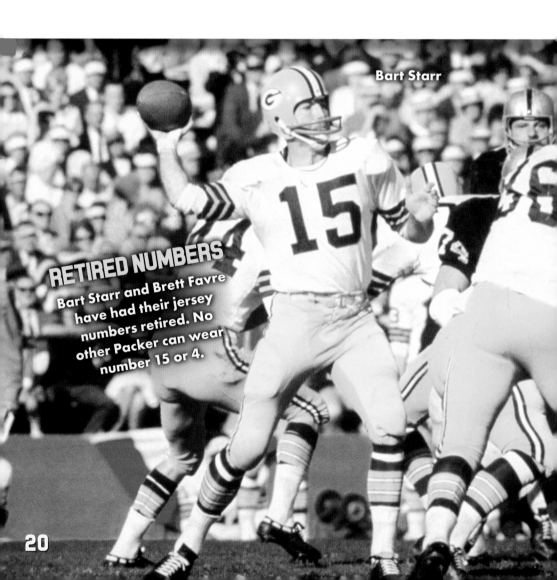

Bart Starr

RETIRED NUMBERS

Bart Starr and Brett Favre have had their jersey numbers retired. No other Packer can wear number 15 or 4.

Aaron Rodgers

Today, Aaron Rodgers keeps the team winning. He helped the Packers win Super Bowl 45.

Football teams need a strong **defense** to do well. **Linebacker** Ray Nitschke helped the Packers win the first two Super Bowls. He is one of the best linebackers of all time.

In Super Bowl 31, **defensive end** Reggie White helped the Packers win. He made three **sacks**. Today, Clay Matthews is the Packers' sack leader.

TEAM GREATS

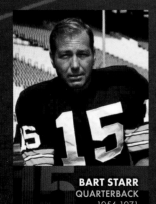

BART STARR
QUARTERBACK
1956-1971

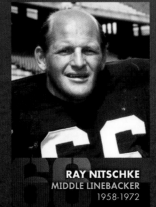

RAY NITSCHKE
MIDDLE LINEBACKER
1958-1972

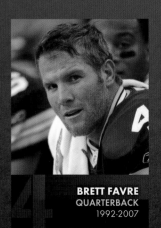

BRETT FAVRE
QUARTERBACK
1992-2007

Clay Matthews

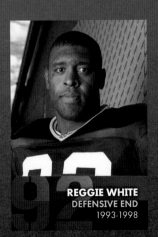

REGGIE WHITE
DEFENSIVE END
1993-1998

AARON RODGERS
QUARTERBACK
2005-PRESENT

CLAY MATTHEWS
LINEBACKER
2009-PRESENT

LAMBEAU LEAP

Packers players celebrate touchdowns with the Lambeau Leap. They jump a six-foot wall into the arms of fans.

The Green Bay Packers are unique in one special way. They are the only NFL team owned by their fans. Fans have been able to buy shares of the team.

Ownership is one main reason Packers fans are so loyal. They are invested in the team's success.

BIKE RIDES

During training camp, kids wait outside the stadium with their bicycles. The players ride the kids' bikes to the nearby practice field.

Wisconsin is known as the "Dairy State." So cheese is a big thing. Packers fans have even been nicknamed "Cheeseheads."

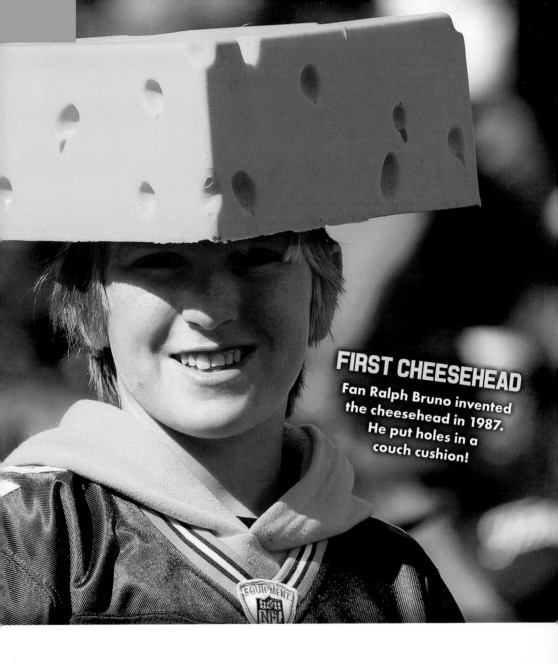

FIRST CHEESEHEAD
Fan Ralph Bruno invented the cheesehead in 1987. He put holes in a couch cushion!

To show support for their state and football team, Packers fans wear foam cheese wedges on their heads. Win or lose, they have pride in "The Green and Gold."

MORE ABOUT THE
PACKERS

Team name:
Green Bay Packers

Team name explained:
Named after the Indian Packing Company, which funded the first season

Nicknames: The Pack, The Green and Gold

Joined NFL: 1921

Conference: NFC

Division: North

Main rivals: Chicago Bears, Minnesota Vikings

Hometown:
Green Bay, Wisconsin

Training camp location:
Lambeau practice fields,
Green Bay, Wisconsin

WISCONSIN

GREEN BAY

Home stadium name: Lambeau Field

Stadium opened: 1957

Seats in stadium: 81,435

Logo: An oval-shaped
G, which stands for
Green Bay

Colors: Green and gold

Name for fan base: Cheeseheads

GLOSSARY

cofounded—worked with one or more people to start a team, company, or other group

conference—a large grouping of sports teams that often play one another

defense—the group of players who try to stop the opposing team from scoring

defensive end—a player on defense whose job is to tackle the player with the ball

division—a small grouping of sports teams that often play one another; usually there are several divisions of teams in a conference.

invested—having great interest in an organization's success

linebacker—a player on defense whose main job is to make tackles and stop passes; a linebacker stands just behind the defensive linemen.

offense—the group of players who try to move down the field and score

playoffs—the games played after the regular NFL season is over; playoff games determine which teams play in the Super Bowl.

professional—a player or team that makes money playing a sport

quarterback—a player on offense whose main job is to throw and hand off the ball

rivalries—long-standing competitions between teams; a rivalry is often between two teams that have played many hard-fought games against each other.

sacks—plays during which a player on defense tackles the opposing quarterback for a loss of yards

shares—portions of ownership in a company

Super Bowl—the championship game for the NFL

wide receiver—a player on offense whose main job is to catch passes from the quarterback

TO LEARN MORE

AT THE LIBRARY

Howell, Brian. *Green Bay Packers*. Mankato, Minn.: Child's World, 2015.

Nagelhout, Ryan. *Aaron Rodgers*. New York, N.Y.: Gareth Stevens Publishing, 2014.

Wittekind, Erika. *What's Great About Wisconsin?* Minneapolis, Minn.: Lerner Publications Company, 2015.

ON THE WEB

Learning more about the Green Bay Packers is as easy as 1, 2, 3.

1. Go to www.factsurfer.com.

2. Enter "Green Bay Packers" into the search box.

3. Click the "Surf" button and you will see a list of related web sites.

With factsurfer.com, finding more information is just a click away.

INDEX